Leith Academy Since 1560

Memories of Leith
Celebrating 450 years

Editor Susan Cook

Published by Leith Academy

Published in 2010 by Leith Academy,
20 Academy Park, Edinburgh EH6 8JQ, Scotland

British Library Cataloguing-in-Publication Data:
A catalogue record of this book is available from the British Library.

ISBN 978-0-9567033-0-9

Printed in Scotland by David Macdonald Ltd.,
25 Rodney Street, Edinburgh EH7 4EL

Leith Academy Since 1560

Memories of Leith
Celebrating 450 years

Contents

FOREWORD

Not many schools get to celebrate their 450th anniversary and it is indeed a privilege to be associated with an institution which has served its community for that length of time. This book contains the comments and reflections of staff and pupils, past and present, as they relate their memories of the school and what it means to them.

The community that is the school has changed hugely over the years and it is fitting that one way that we have chosen to celebrate our auspicious birthday is through events that aim at embracing the diversity that makes up the school population today. These events and experiences will hopefully contribute to the memories of the future.

People who buy this book will most likely be those who have an association with the school and who will have their own memories. I hope that the collection of memories and observations printed here will, in their own way, add to yours.

The school's motto is one that serves both institution and individual well. The school has indeed persevered over the last four and a half centuries in catering for its ever-changing clientele in an ever-changing world. Many of its pupils have gone on to persevere in their own lives, having been set up to do so by the education they received. There is much for us to be proud of in that.

Here's to the next 450 years!

Jack Simpson, Head Teacher, Leith Academy

Leith Academy 1945

Leith Academy Class 2A1 June 1945

Sketch of the History of Leith Academy
by Alexander Mackay
(Former teacher of Leith Academy)

The Management of the School (1795 – 1896)

The Trustees paid no salary to the teachers appointed by them. These teachers depended entirely on the fees paid by the pupils. The two teachers appointed by the Kirk Session received, as had always been the case, a salary in addition to the fees. Mr Bayne's salary amounted to £36 a year. The two new teachers appointed in his place in 1826 each received £25 per annum "in consideration of the present state of the school," that is, in view of the decreased attendance of pupils. Each teacher paid a rent for his room to the Trustees, a charge which was met by the Session in the case of the Latin and English teachers. The rent was originally fixed at one guinea per annum, but later on the teachers who occupied the two class rooms on the ground floor were called upon to pay £5 per annum. The rent question was a sore point with the teachers. In addition to paying rent, the teachers had to pay for all repairs other than those necessary to keep the building wind and water tight, and, until a janitor was appointed, they were also responsible for the cleaning of the class rooms, stairs and passages. This responsibility does not seem to have been taken very seriously by at least one of the teachers regarding whose half of the lobby a colleague complained, "It is as thick of dust at this moment as if Mount Vesuvius had showered ashes upon it since the days of Pliny the Younger." On

Leith Academy Primary School children attend the church next door to the school for an assembly (circa 1947)

Class 3A2, 1952   Teacher Mr Harry Milne

the appointment of a janitor to the school, the teachers were required to collect sixpence per quarter from each pupil, and to pay over the same to the janitor.

The school had no fixed curriculum, parents being free to choose what classes they pleased for their children, and therefore all the pupils did not pass through the different departments. There is no record of the number of pupils attending the classes of the Mathematical Master and the Arithmetic Master, but Mr Bayne had 120 boys in his Latin classes in 1811, the year in which these classes were most numerously attended, and in the same year Mr Foggo had 90 boys and 25 girls, 115 pupils in all, in his English classes. At no time do the pupils seem to have exceeded 250 in number. Between 1825 and 1835 the greatest number of scholars was 250, and the smallest 160.

In 1863 with a view to improving its organisation, the Town Council made a change in the constitution of the school. They appointed a Rector, and to him was committed the appointment of teachers, and the general control and management of the school. They, however, paid no salary either to the Rector or to his assistants, and indeed even expected the Rector to bear part of the expense of keeping up the school. The Rector's income was entirely dependent on the fees, out of which he paid his assistants, and he permitted anyone to attend any class or number of classes in the school. Pupils might thus take lessons in French, or in German or in drawing, or in music, without attending any class in any other department. In fact, the school was a large private adventure school, and the Rector very reasonably made what he could out of it in the way that paid best.

The subjects taught were English, Latin, Greek, French, German, Mathematics, Book-keeping, Drawing, Needlework, and Music. There were seven assistant masters and three assistant mistresses. The majority of the scholars attended the English, writing and arithmetic classes. In 1867 of the 198 pupils on the roll 14 were taking Latin, 25 French, 4 German, 22 music, and 11 sewing.

In 1896 the High School buildings, which had become utterly inadequate for their purpose, were pulled down and were replaced by a school which now forms the Primary Leith Academy, the cost being quite ten times that of the original structure. The coins and documents which had been placed in the urn on the occasion of the laying of the foundation stone in 1804 were recovered during the process of demolition and are now displayed in the headmaster's room. One of the parchments gives the name of the original Trustees of the school

Leith Academy 1931

The new school was formally declared open by Lord Provost Whitson on 12 January

'Tattie Picking' at Kelso, 1952

Leith Academy Secondary School - - 1952

1931, in the presence of an audience which completely filled the large hall of the school. The Lord Provost traced briefly the history of the school through the centuries, and congratulated the rector, staff and pupils that they had now school buildings of the most up-to-date and adequate description. So great had been the pressure on the accommodation of the Academy for many years past that the main building had proved utterly inadequate to its needs, and basements, workshops, huts, a corrugated iron structure, and a church hall, had all been requisitioned to provide classrooms. That state of matters was now a thing of the past, and the splendidly appointed building in which they were met that day would enable the work of the school to be carried on in peace and comfort under ideal conditions.

The school, which is three storeys in height, is built of brick on a steel frame, and is faced with stone. It consists of five blocks or wings grouped round a central hall. Corridors, from which the classrooms open, circulate on the inner side of all five blocks.

There are 25 ordinary classrooms, all with a southern exposure, 6 physics and chemistry laboratories, 3 art rooms, 3 craft rooms, 3 domestic science rooms, 2 geography rooms, a music room and a library. The school hall which can be divided into two

Leith Academy   1926 -1927

Leith Academy   Class Junior 1 1928 -1929

Leith Academy   Primary School 1931 -1932

gymnasia, is provided with a stage fully equipped with all the appliances necessary for the performance of dramatic plays.

The school with about 1000 pupils on the roll, and a staff of 45 teachers, makes provision for two main types of pupils. For scholars taking a three years' course there are General, Technical, and Domestic Courses, these being especially suitable for pupils who intend to engage in commerce, business, or industry. A certificate, the "Day school Certificate (Higher)," is issued by the Scottish Education Department to pupils who have satisfactorily completed such a course. For pupils who undertake a Secondary Course of at least five years' duration, there are courses suitable for those who are preparing for the higher branches of industry and commerce, or who propose to enter a profession. These courses lead to the award of the Leaving certificate, which qualifies for entrance to the University and to various professions.

Addendum by Jack Simpson (current Headteacher)

Leith Academy 1991 to present (2010)

The Leith Academy we know today was opened in May 1991, following a long campaign by parents, pupils and staff. Regarded as one of the finest school buildings in Europe, it is a fitting testament to the long and proud history of education in Leith.

LEITH ACADEMY MAGAZINE
QUATERCENTENARY NUMBER

By courtesy of "Evening News"

The Lord and Lady Provost greet the Rector and Mrs Drummond at the Civic Reception which inaugurated the Quatercentenary Celebrations.

1560 - 1960

EDITORIAL.

The School is celebrating its four hundred years and for the last forty this magazine has mirrored the life and fortunes of the Academy, for it was in December 1919 that the F.P.'s Association issued the first school magazine, under the title of *Leith Academy — Past and Present*, a title retained until December 1926.

QUATERCENTENARY CELEBRATIONS

The origins of Leith Academy lie so far back in history that we cannot be sure when or by whom the School was founded. We do know, however, that in 1560 the School became, in a very real sense, the school of Leith. The association begun in that year between the School and the community has persisted and flourished despite many vicissitudes, so that today we can look back over four centuries of unbroken service to the people of Leith.

This was clearly an occasion for thanksgiving and rejoicing, and the School's present Governors, the Town Council of the City of Edinburgh, shared this view and decided that the occasion should be marked by a special programme of celebrations.

PROGRAMME OF EVENTS

Monday, 30th May—Civic Reception.

Thursday, 2nd June—Treeplanting ceremony.

Saturday, 4th June—School Sports.

Sunday, 5th June—Service of Thanksgiving.

Tuesday, 7th June—Open School.

Thursday, 9th June—Commemoration Day.

Saturday, 18th June—Commemoration Dinner of the Former Pupils' Association.

Monday, 20th June }
Friday, 24th June } Pageant of Leith.

450th Diversity Celebrations

Leith Academy is a Community School which is proud to be known as "a school for the whole Community." Through its Adult Education and Community Programme, and its programme for school pupils in S1- S6, Leith Academy celebrates the richness and diversity of its entire community. The school goes to great lengths to provide an environment that is inclusive of people with disabilities and pupils with additional support needs. The school has a roll of 920 pupils from 32 different nationalities. The school promotes active and responsible citizenship through a stimulating and varied programme of themed assemblies and tutor group activities such as Diversity, Holocaust Memorial Day, Ethos and Values, Multi –culturalism and enhances links through sharing photographs, writing letters to pupils and teacher exchanges with our link school in Malawi. The Pupil Council is an active force in the school and it was a suggestion from the pupils on the Pupil Council which led to the enormous success of our Diversity celebrations which bring together many cultures from within the local community in the various events run throughout the year.

The pupils have been encouraged to become active citizens within their local community and in promoting good links between the school and community through their pro-active approach in coordinating and jointly running an International Market Place on the Diversity Days at Leith Academy. Their enterprising approach, which involved going out and speaking to local businesses, has ensured a wide selection of stalls highlighting the true diversity in our local and wider community. The pupils secured representation of foods and goods stalls from around the globe; Africa, Poland, India, China, USA, Italy, Scotland and stalls representing humanitarian causes such as 'Purple Pinkie'. Fair-trade and Show Racism the Red Card also have attended to raise awareness of global world issues and heightened our awareness of our role in supporting these causes through our every day actions. Along with staff and pupils, the engagement of members of the local and wider community we have actively promoted a unified approach to the celebration of diversity.

With 32 different nationalities at Leith Academy one of the most salient ways of developing pupils' understanding of diversity has been to allow them to educate each other. To this end pupils have devised and showcase their performances at our 'Diversity Show'. This has given them an opportunity to teach other pupils about their culture and customs through different media such as dance, song, poetry etc. There have also been contributions from the wider community at these shows such as Jamie Andrew, the mountaineer who spoke about 'Perseverance in the face of adversity' and recounted the loss of his hands and feet in a mountaineering accident. He talked about 'being different' but how this difference could be positive and his story of his own and others acceptance of his disability gave a powerful message and was very thought provoking to all present. Janice Gilani (former Dux 1967) spoke of her time in Iraq and Ian Gilmour, the school Chaplain, reflected on days gone by.

The shows have incorporated Scottish Country dancers from associate primaries, performers from Leith Theatre Company, fashion shows featuring national dress from around the world, Thai and Bollywood dancers. Our most recent Diversity show featured a song called 'Stand Tall' which was written and sung by our pupils. Moving with modern times, one of our pupils devised and performed a Diversity rap in his national Pakistani dress. Our Polish pupils have performed traditional Polish folk songs and our shows culminated in our entire audiences joining together in a rendition of Auld Lang Syne sung in Spanish, Polish, Gaelic and Scots.

These events have combined to celebrate all aspects of diversity – age, disability, social class, faith, belief, ethnicity and sexuality – which allowed pupils to develop an understanding of different traditions, beliefs and cultures and develop informed ethical views.

With the support of our school community we have been able to offer over 30 Diversity workshops for pupils to opt into which give them a wider knowledge of the various cultures around the world. These workshops have included; Japanese Culture and Customs, Chinese Calligraphy and Indian Cookery, Gaelic Football, Salsa Dancing and Henna Hand Painting. These workshops have been run by local businesses, the community school tutors and parents/carers. These workshops, along with the International Market Place and Show, have had a significant impact in raising awareness of the fluidity of cultures across the globe and the richness and value that living in a multi-cultural society brings with it. Pupils have developed life skills and a deeper understanding of diversity and are better prepared for success in the wider world. The school and community have moved from toleration and acceptance of diversity to embracing it. Positive relationships across the local community have developed.

As part of our year long approach to Diversity and our 450th Celebrations we ran a photographic competition, where pupils, staff and members of the local and wider community contributed photographs from around the world featuring people, landscapes, buildings, animals etc. which allowed others to gain an insight into the various countries, cultures and customs around the world. In addition, we also ran an images of Leith competition to encourage pupils and others to explore and appreciate their own local community. The images received, over 350, demonstrated that our community is truly a global one; many of the photographs were submitted from pupils and members of the wider community who had spent many of their years living in other countries (some from birth) or working in countries such as Zambia, Tanzania and Albania as volunteers. Many of the images of Leith photographs represented our multi-cultural community as the pictures taken were of shops, restaurants and the various cultural festivals celebrated such as Diwali and Chinese New Year. These photographs, judged by the Evening News and shown here, have allowed pupils to gain information about other countries through the eyes of others. It has inspired them to want to go and visit other countries in the future; to learn more about them as their discussions with the pupils and members of the community who took the images have shared their experiences of their time in these countries. This has developed our pupils understanding of the international dimension of citizenship.

The winning image of Leith was by Dale Neish, a pupil at Leith Academy, who captured a snowy scene at Leith Links.

The winning image from Around the World was submitted by a former pupil, Liam Anderson, and was taken in Zambia when he was working with South Leith Parish Church building dormitories for pupils. The picture is of a brother and sister.

The Leith Academy Story
By Reverend Ian Gilmour (South Leith Parish Church)

The story begins like this. Once, long ago in a place not far away, a group of adventurous Leithers devised a cunning plan. The idea was to engage and enthuse children in learning.

Leith Academy has a great story. I'm delighted that Mr Simpson has given me the privilege of sharing a bit of it with you. It is a story of pupils gaining knowledge; of committed teachers; of adaptation across centuries.

This is one of the oldest Schools in Scotland. When the school began only around 1% of the people in Leith could read or write. None of them learn these skills in Leith. No need for a library. The major school in Edinburgh refused Leith people access, even if they could pay!

Leith Academy has been called many names including Leith High School, Leith Grammar and before that a branch called the Sang School (also known as the Vulgar or Music School).

South Leith Church and the school have had rich connection since the first day. The Grammar School stood for a while in the Kirkgate within the present churchyard, remaining until 1806 when it was transferred to the Links and became Leith Academy.

For a long time the teaching language in this school was not in English, it was Latin. We even know the names of the books pupils studied.

The teachers were always committed but in the past they had some different responsibilities, for example, cleaning! Now some teachers were more enthusiastic about clearing up than others "Mr Baynes half of the lobby....is as thick of dust as if Mount Vesuvius has showered ashes upon it."

Why were the pupils educated? To develop their minds, spirit and discipline. Always a strong relationship between school and the workplace. The Trade incorporations such as Seafarers, Shoemakers and Hammermen were supportive of the school. The Port of Leith has a proud history of trade. Of industrial output producing ships, biscuits, ropes and bottling whisky.

Back in the 1800s barrels of whisky were stored in the School and apparently some of the boys drank the whisky using straws.

You may ask what about the girls? The first female pupils came into Leith Academy under the Education Act 1872 when the School Boards were set up.

I thought you may wish to hear about one of the most difficult periods and the problem was the heidie!

The year is 1729 and the headmaster of the school was Mr Thomas Kirkwood. There had been some hesitation in giving him an appointment of so great importance to the youth of the town. Quite often to appoint a new head, two Professors from Edinburgh University, two ministers plus the head of the Royal High School would be invited to interview candidates. In this case they had been impressed by fair words and promises by Mr Kirkwood. Unfortunately his words and his deeds didn't match up.

He was I quote, "a friend of publicans, one who indulged ... but too well in the cup that clears today of past regrets and future fears" - "The headmaster didn't always turn up himself, nor was he strict in requiring the boys to be punctual, and he did not allow his assistant to correct or punish the boys in his absence!" No strict timekeeping, I can see that might appeal to some here. However, the school fell into manifest decay under his control, and parents delayed sending their children to Leith Academy because of his conversation and behaviour.

It was only after him the school began flourishing again under the care of another head.

Many tales over 450 years and the most interesting ones are about people. People who worked hard and fought for this community with vigour and courage. Their intellects sharpened because of the teaching received here. Such stalwarts lived out the school's marvellous motto Persevere.

Of the many buildings used 3 remain. Looking out on Leith Links - It's now Leith Primary, then at the corner of Duke Street the 1931 building and this magnificent building of 1991, except of course, upstairs on our rare hot summer days.

Schools are about commitment to society ....what will pupils become...every type of work or profession a possibility. Pupils from here have reached many high positions.

Today we have excellent facilities, teachers, materials and numerous opportunities.

But how you will make your mark? How will we read about the pupils of today in the papers over the next period of years?

I am proud to be a tiny part of this story and I hope you are too.

Sunny Leith

Rajni Punn
EAL Teacher at Leith Academy for 19 years

Leith is a unique and beautiful part of the city. It is friendly and welcoming with a vibrant multicultural community which is ever changing. Over the years it has rapidly changed with the most recent communities coming from Eastern Europe. Historically, the Italian and Indian community had been a well established part of Leith since the 1940s with a Sikh temple at Mill Lane and a Hindu temple at Duke Place. In fact the Indian and Italian restaurants in Leith are the best, allowing the Leith area to represent most of the different communities found in the city. The shop fronts on Leith Walk open the eyes of Edinburgh to superb displays of exotic fruits, vegetables and spices as shops proudly display and sell goods from across the globe.

Restaurants and local shops in Leith have adapted well to the demands of the community around them and it is not unusual to see Haggis placed next to a Samoa or Spring roll in a local shop fridge in Leith Walk. It is evident from the fusion of food found in Leith Walk that the locals have welcomed the new generation that make up Leith. Haggis Pakoras and Haggis Pizzas are but a few delights that have been created from this diverse culture and the local people have embraced these tantalising, tasteful delights with enthusiasm to make them part of the Scottish culture.

The most celebrated time for Leith is when the various communities are happy to share and promote their cultural inheritance during the Edinburgh Mela. Here the opportunity is given for the various communities to come together to celebrate their diversity and this is most prominent during the Festival held in our very own heart of Leith –at the Links. It is in these organised community social gatherings that the people of Leith show their true colours. This provides the community of Leith with the opportunity to come together in traditional dress and celebrate their diversity whilst playing host to tourists and friends. The opportunity here is taken to demonstrate identity and cultural inheritance to the young children of Leith, raising awareness of cultural diversity and good citizenship.

Finally it is no wonder Leith is called 'Sunny Leith' because the people radiate the warmth of the sun. The festivals, the taste of traditional food, being absorbed in culture, music and hospitality makes up Leith because these functions welcome anyone who enjoys community gatherings and especially if they would like to be part of the Leith Community in Edinburgh. I'm proud to be part of the Leith Community.

Rajni's Chickpea Curry and Savoury Cumin and Onion Rice.

Chickpea Curry

Ingredients
2/3 tbsp oil
2/3 large onions, chopped
2 garlic clove, crushed
¼ tsp salt
½ tsp cumin powder
¼ tsp coriander powder

¼ tsp turmeric powder
¼ tsp red chilli powder
1 tin of chopped Tomatoes
1 x 400g/14oz can chickpeas, drained and rinsed
5cm/2in piece root ginger, grated

1 tsp garam masala, pinch of dry fenugreek and fresh coriander leaves.
Method
1. Heat a deep saucepan - add the oil followed by the onions and garlic.
2. Fry the mixture till the onions are caramelised. Then add the salt, cumin, coriander, turmeric and red chilli powders. Mix for a minute and tip in the tomato. Cook the sauce until it begins to thicken or when you can see the oil appearing on top.
3. Add 1/2 cups of water and stir. Then tip in the chickpeas and mix. Mash a few of the chickpeas while cooking. Cover and simmer for five minutes. Then add the ginger and the garam masala and fenugreek leaves. Cook for 5mins. Finish off with chopped coriander.

Cumin and Onion Rice

Ingredients:
1   Cup of Basmati Rice
2   1 tsp of Cumin
3   Pinch of Salt
4   1 large Onion
5   2/3 tbsp of Oil
Method
1   Heat oil in pan and add cumin seed for 1min. Place sliced onion and caramelise until golden brown.
2   Put washed basmati rice and salt in pan with 2 cups of boiled water.
3   Cook on lowest heat and stir only at the beginning and then leave.
4   Once cooked leave for 5 min. to steam.

Vegetarian haggis pakoras with a duo of chutneys

A traditional recipe for pakoras combining Scottish and Punjabi cuisines, served with mint & apple and rhubarb chutneys.

RECIPE DETAILS
Servings: 8
Prep time: 10min
Cook time: 1hr 20min
Dish type: Starters
Difficulty: Medium
Cuisine: British, Vegetarian
Chef: Contestant chef
Programme: Britain's Best Dish

Ingredients
For the pakoras:
250g gram flour
1tbsp garam masala
1tbsp dried Fenugreek leaves
1tsp Ajwan seeds
Salt, as required
Chilli powder as required
3tbsp yoghurt
Water – as required
Local Scottish vegetable Haggis
2 large British potatoes
1 large white onion
3 fresh green chillies
2 - 3 leaves green cabbage
Sunflower or olive oil for frying

For the rhubarb chutney:
2 - 3 sticks rhubarb
1tsp Nigella seeds
½tsp freshly ground black pepper
½tsp red chilli powder
½tsp ground roasted cumin seeds
¼tsp salt
½tsp marsala
2 – 3tbsp sugar
2tbsp water
6 or 7 cloves

For the mint and apple chutney:
1 large green cooking apple
1 large onion
Bunch fresh mint
Bunch fresh coriander
Juice of one lemon
3 fresh green chillies, chopped
2 tomatoes, chopped
1 tsp ground black pepper
½tsp salt
½tsp marsala

For the grated salad:
Carrot, cucumber, red onions, iceberg lettuce

Preparation
1. For the rhubarb chutney, wash and chop the rhubarb. Place in a pan with the other ingredients. Bring to the boil then reduce the heat and simmer for 5 - 6 minutes.
2. Once cooked remove from the heat and leave to cool for 15 to 20 minutes. Place in a jar or freezer to quicken the cooling process.
3. For the mint and apple chutney, peel and chop the apple and onion. Wash the mint leaves and coarsely chop the coriander. Place into a blender with the lemon juice and remaining ingredients.
4. Blend together until the consistency resembles a chutney. Put the mixture into a jar and keep cool.
5. To make the pakora batter, put all the dry ingredients into a large bowl and mix. Add the yoghurt and water gradually and mix the batter until smooth but not thick. Leave aside for 5-10 minutes.
6. Steam the haggis for 20 minutes, then leave to cool for 10 minutes.
7. Peel wash and grate the potatoes. Peel and slice the onions and finely chop the chillies and cabbage. Mix all the vegetables into the batter.
8. Heat the oil in a frying pan for 5 minutes. Scoop out a small tablespoon of haggis and place it in the batter to coat.
9. Place the mixture into hot oil and fry for 2-3 minutes until golden-brown. Turn repeatedly to ensure even frying. Once cooked, remove from the pan and place onto a kitchen towel to dry. Prepare the salad.
10. Serve the pakoras with the chutneys and grated salad.

I Love Leith
By **Bina Bhandari** (S6)

My name is Bina Bhandari. I am from Nepal. I came to Leith in October 2006 with my parents. When I was on the way to Scotland I was happy to see new places and meet new people but on the other hand I was sad because I was missing my friends in Nepal. I was worried about what the weather was going to be like, what kind of people there was in Scotland. When I arrived here I was very confused because everything was different from my country. It was very cold and snow was falling. I had never seen snow in my country so it was interesting to see. Everything looked white as if someone had decorated it with flour. It was really beautiful to see.

When I walked around Leith I heard people talking but I couldn't understand English. When I was new I did not like anything but after a few months I stared to like Leith because I made some friends and visited all around the Leith area.

When I joined Leith Academy I was happy because there were so many pupils and teachers in school all were friendly and helpful. I had problems with the language because I could not understand what my friends were asking about.

When I first went to buy food in Tesco in Leith I was confused because I was thinking that the food here was the same as my country but I was wrong. There were so many different foods that I was confused about what to buy. All the foods looked nicely displayed but I had no idea what they were. Then I saw some Asian shops and I knew the food in this shop would be like the food in my country. Later I wanted to try some Scottish food so I went back to Tesco to buy something that was Scottish. I asked the shop assistant and she showed me Scotch broth. I took it home and realised it was very tasty and like our lentil dahl that we make in Nepal. In Nepal I enjoyed eating mangoes a lot so I was surprised to see mangoes in a shop on Leith Walk. But these mangoes were different, not sweet but a bit tangy. They were from Brazil.

The people of Leith have made me feel welcome. I miss Nepal but I do like living in Leith. This is my home now and my family live here.

Asian Mela – Pilrig Park

Fascinating, colourful, echoing fireworks
Inspiring, achievable desires
Coming out on nights like this!
Hurrying, rushing heavy footsteps
Pacing eagerly!
Emphatic, loud; people
Hugging and celebrating!
Fierce, enormous spirals
Aiming to shoot up to the sky!
Joyous, sweet voices
Singing to the melody of the music!
Running, playful children
Jumping and clapping their hands!
Kicking, raging, rioting people
Drunk with happiness!
Smashed, bright bottles of wine
Staining the grass
Giganitic big swaying trees
Fill the world with greenery!
The great wind and ambience
Flickers through my hair!
Thousands of eyes
Can only see love spreading around me
This is why I'm proud to be a Muslim
This is why I'm proud to live in Leith!

SHEEBA ZAHIR (1.7)

Janice Gilani
(née Mackenzie)
Dux 1967

Janice kindly gave a talk for us at our recent Diversity Day on 11th February 2010. This is what she said:

If anyone had told me, forty years ago, that I would be standing here today speaking at an event on diversity, I would have said they were mad! I was born and brought up in Leith, went to school at the old Leith Academy across in the Links, and then straight on to Edinburgh University. No gap years in those days! My only claim to any experience of diversity then was that my father was a highlander, from Dornoch; my friends thought he spoke with a funny accent and we went on holiday every year to darkest Sutherland.

Once I left university, I'd travelled quite a bit and thought I knew a fair bit of the world by the time I met my future husband. Even so, I had to go and look up Baghdad in an atlas when he told me where he came from. Yes, I knew about Mesopotamia, the Tigris and Euphrates, but Iraq and Iran meant nothing to me.

I knew very little about Islam either, apart from the fact that Muslims pray several times a day, facing Mecca, and that the men can legally have four wives. My friends knew even less, imagining I would be going to live in a tent in the desert, wear a black cloak, cover my face and ride a camel. None of this, of course, was true. The Baghdad of the seventies was a modern, progressive city, about the size of London, with two universities and the younger women, at least, were well-educated, held down jobs, and followed European fashions.

Still, nothing could have prepared me for the strangeness of my first few days in Iraq. What I remember most is the terrific heat, although it was only April; the mosquitoes which enjoyed feasting on Scottish blood; and the traffic which was crazy, noisy and interspersed with donkeys and small herds of goats – but no camels.

So what can I tell you in a few minutes about how different life in Iraq was? I could tell you about the problems I had at first learning to shop from open street markets with un-familiar fruit and vegetables and no convenience foods ; I could talk about how I struggled with the language – the strange alphabet, reading from right to left, the fact that the language spoken around me every day was very different from the

Standard Arabic used by the media; or I could describe the difficulties and delights of Ramadan, the month of fasting. But you might be more interested in hearing a little of what life was like for teenagers – what your lives would be like – in Iraq. For a start, you wouldn't all be sitting here together now. After primary, boys and girls go to separate schools.

The school week is six days, with only Friday off and classes start early and end at 1.30pm. This may sound great but, for most of the year, it's too hot after that time to do anything but go home and have a siesta. Weekday evenings would be spent doing homework and perhaps watching a little television or playing computer games, if your parents would let you. Discipline at home, and at school, is strict.

On Fridays, the boys might go to the mosque with their fathers or perhaps meet their friends to play football or ride bikes. Girls would be expected to help with household chores or might be allowed to visit friends who lived nearby. Evenings would find the whole family out visiting, strolling in the park, or sitting in one of the popular open-air cafes along the riverside. Winter, when the weather is kinder, is the time for family picnics in the countryside or trips to see one of the many rich archaeological sites like Babylon or Nineveh. So much for your social lives!

Education is all important. While it isn't compulsory to complete the six years of secondary school, prospects are bleak for those who don't. There is no unemployment benefit and boys not in full-time education are called for national service at sixteen. After the final 6th year exams, the Board of Education decides, on the basis of your grades, whether you continue to college or university and even what subject you study. Only the lucky few with top grades are allowed any personal choice. So it's not uncommon for anxious parents to pay for extra tuition for their children.

I'm sure all this sounds very different from your own lives, but young Iraqis, in general, were quite content with their lives and enjoyed the security of strong family ties. Problems of drinking, drugs, vandalism and violence were almost unheard of. Neighbours looked out for each other as a matter of course. As a "foreigner" I might easily have been left out of this community, but, in fact, people went out of their way to include me. People were genuinely interested in me and in finding out about life in the UK. Their knowledge of life here, based on the American films they saw on television, was as flawed as mine had been of the Muslim world, so we learned a lot from each other.

Historically, Baghdad is sometimes referred to as Madinat al-Salaam, City of Peace, as, during the rule of the caliphs, Baghdad was a great centre of learning. That seems quite ironic now. Of the twenty-one years I lived in Iraq, fifteen were spent either at war or with rationing and sanctions. Life had always been hard for the ordinary people, but now it became even more difficult with people struggling to keep their families fed.

When Saddam Hussein invaded Kuwait and the United States and Britain threatened war, I suddenly found myself in the strange position of being the "enemy within." Even at that time, when racial or religious hatred might have been expected, I was unfailingly treated with respect and kindness.

While I would never recommend that anyone go out and live in a war zone, my time in Iraq was a great education, one I could never have gained in any university. It helped me to appreciate what we have here in the UK, and what we have lost, to understand more about the far-reaching consequences of war, and to value and respect other beliefs and cultures.

I'm proud to know that my old school celebrates diversity. I hope that you will all take some food for thought away from the day.

Alastair Chisholm

Dux 1971 and teacher at Leith Academy for 32 years

Alastair started Leith Academy Primary School in 1958 and was in Primary 2 when he took part in the 400th anniversary celebrations in 1960. After progressing to Leith Academy Secondary School in 1965, Alistair won the award for 'Initiative' in his 1st year and in 1971, was named Dux of the school and was awarded the Dux medal. Alastair was very proud that he attended an institution that was even older than Edinburgh University.

As a pupil at Leith Academy, Alastair was a Prefect. He was a keen singer and sang bass in both the school and Edinburgh Secondary Schools Choir. Alastair also liked playing chess and taught both of his brothers, Kenneth (runner up Dux, 1974) and Douglas (Dux, 1980) to play. Alastair took part in many of the Gilbert and Sullivan productions run by the school, both as a performer and latterly, organising the lighting for these. In 1971 Alastair had a brush with the law, when he played the foreman, as he sung in Trial by Jury. Alastair was an active member of the Literary and Debating Society, always able to get his points across clearly, and he continued his passion for this in joining Edinburgh University's debating team when he went there to study as a student. Kenneth was also a Prefect and Depute Head Boy. He recalls being invited to the then Headteacher's room, Douglas Mackay, who spoke to him in his office and said "I am considering appointing you as Depute Head Boy" to which Kenneth exclaimed "Are you sure"? Kenneth thought that you could only be given this accolade if you were in the sports teams or were highly intellectual. However Kenneth was a very good role model and was musically talented, being given school colours for his playing of the French horn in both the school and Edinburgh Schools Orchestra. He also describes his pleasure in being invited on a few occasions to play in Elliott Wardlaw's Glenn Miller style Big Band. Kenneth was also runner-up Dux in 1974. Douglas was not selected as a Prefect, although he said that he had played rugby for a while, but felt that Prefects in his day were predominantly selected from the sporting teams. He recalls Mr Mackay's catchphrase at assemblies on a Monday morning "we need more boys playing rugby………on Saturdays".

On one occasion Alastair actually taught Douglas for a physics class. Both believed that this had been arranged by a rather mischievous school management. It certainly appealed to Alastair's sense of fun even if it caused Douglas some embarrassment at the time.

In 1980, Douglas became Dux Boy, keeping the family tradition alive, and allowing Alastair and himself to tease Ken, a mere runner-up, on countless family occasions and curry nights.

Kenneth and Douglas have a few funny memories of their time at Leith Academy. Douglas and some friends in his class set off a fire extinguisher one day in the PE games hall and then tried to cover their tracks by using the gymnastic mats to soak up the water. Needless to say their plan didn't work and they were caught red handed! Kenneth remembers his History teacher, Mr Aitken, who was a bit hard of hearing towards the end of his career, picking up the phone in the classroom when members of his class simulated a phone ringing. He took a while to catch on to the fact that nobody seemed to be on the end of the line when he picked it up and he had been set up.

In terms of inspirational teachers, Kenneth and Douglas highlight two teachers who had proved to be very motivating for all 3 brothers; Thomas Beattie, who was Head of Physics at Leith Academy and former Dux in 1941 (his son, Euan, also became Dux at Leith Academy) and John Young (Maths teacher). Thomas Beattie made Physics really interesting and invoked in pupils a quest for knowledge about this area. He also helped arrange a trip to the International Youth Science fortnight in London, which both Alastair and Kenneth had attended – with Kenneth even getting to meet Sir Christopher

SCHOOL PROJECT . . . NO. 1

Pupils of Leith Academy and their mathematics master, Mr J. Young—who has to " chase them out of school " at nights—at work on the television monitor. They are (left)—Douglas Black (18), Andrew Jack (15), Alastair Chisholm (18) and his brother Kenneth (15), and John Dalgleish.

Cockerell who invented the hovercraft. John Young was particularly inspirational for Alastair and used to run a computing club after school and the brothers believe that it was John Young's vested interest in this area that allowed Leith Academy to be the designated school to receive one of the first computers in the United Kingdom (which had all of 200 words storage capacity). John Young eventually left Leith Academy to take up a lectureship in Computing Science at Moray House

Post school

After leaving Leith Academy Alastair went on to Edinburgh University to study Physics where he graduated with an honours degree. Having always wanted to be a teacher, after being inspired by Thomas Beattie and John Young, he went to Moray House to train as a Physics teacher. Both Kenneth and Douglas had recognised Alastair's flair when as younger brothers he used to give them encouragement and help with their homework. It was natural that Alastair would proceed to a career in teaching. After a year's teaching in Livingston Alastair found his dream job teaching Physics back at Leith Academy. Although Alastair's first subject was Physics, he also had to teach general science. Kenneth and Douglas recall Alastair's horror regarding an aspect of the Biology course he had to teach to pupils – inflating a sheep's lung by blowing in to a tube. This was a huge undertaking for a man who would cross the road when he stumbled upon a butcher's shop as it made him feel squeamish!

Alastair had always been passionate about computers and designed and built his own computer before PC's were invented. This was a truly amazing piece of engineering at the time. Wishing to pursue this interest and pass this knowledge and interest onto pupils he decided to re-train in Computing Studies, which he then taught at Leith Academy. This love of computing, instilled in these three young boys at school, has continued into their career pathways now, with Kenneth lecturing in Computing Science at Napier University and Douglas becoming a micro-electronics engineer working on many computer chips at Inmos, ARM and currently ADI.

Leith Academy

As a teacher Alastair was dedicated to the school and truly valued education. He was committed to ensuring pupils achieved of their best not only in his subject but in the

wider school as a whole. He also willingly gave of his time to support the life and work of the school through his membership of school and national development groups such as GLOW and in his participation in staff pantomimes; sponsored walks and Diversity celebrations. Outwith teaching Alastair was active in politics, becoming vice-President of the Edinburgh University Students Association at the time Gordon Brown was the student rector. Alastair was an active member of the Liberal Party and helping Rev Elizabeth Wardlaw (the councillor for Leith Links) and other candidates organise elections in Leith. To Alastair, politics was fun. Alastair was also a keen war gamer and member of the South East Scotland War Games Club. He enjoyed going to conventions across the UK with his friends, especially Dave Douglas a fellow computer studies teacher.

For many staff who joined Alastair for lunch we will never forget his little idiosyncrasies – he always ate his main course first, followed by his soup and dessert. His reasoning for this being that the soup stayed hottest the longest – words spoken by a true scientist! Alastair also liked to round off his lunch by joining colleagues in the staffroom or staff base and enjoying a diet coke (a privilege as fizzy juice is now banned at the school for all pupils).

Alastair has been a great inspiration to many, as Thomas Beattie and John Young were to him. He dedicated most of his life to Leith Academy, both as a pupil and as a teacher, until his untimely death in July 2010. He will be fondly remembered by staff, pupils and parents alike.

Kenneth Chisholm 1961 – 1974

Douglas Chisholm 1967 – 1980

John Nicholson (Jock) Wilson

Leith Academy's (and Britain's) most decorated D-Day veteran

Born: 7th September, 1903, in Edinburgh

Died: 29th September, 2008, in Dunbar

Jock was born on September 7th 1903 and lived to be 105 years old and was Britain's oldest and most decorated D-Day veteran. After leaving Leith Academy at the age of 14, Jock worked for a short time at McNiven and Cameron's, the makers of Waverley Pens. Later on in his teenage years Jock joined the Scottish Horse Guard. He married Lily (née Ross) in October 1934, after meeting her at a tea party at a ballroom in Seafield. They went on to have one daughter together, Joyce.

When World War II started Jock did not expect to be conscripted as he had retired from the army some years earlier. However Jock was called up in 1941, at the age of 38, and joined the 79th Regiment of the Royal Artillery. He was assigned to the radio division. When his daughter Joyce was only two weeks old, Jock flew out to France to fight against Germany. He landed at Juno Beach on June 6th, 1944, where his unit were amongst the first group of soldiers to land in Normandy. Jock acted as an artillery observer and guided his unit's guns in their bombardment of German defensive positions. It was his unit's radio transmissions, which gave detailed information about the enemy's movements, and which allowed the allies to decide where to deploy troops. Jock was later awarded the Military Medal for his performance in Normandy, and later in Belgium, the Netherlands and Germany.

After the war Jock returned home to Scotland and worked for many years as a printer (until 1976). He spent much of his spare time with his wife, daughter and supporting his local football club, Hibernian. Jock's wife, Lily, died in 1964 and shortly after this he moved from Edinburgh to Dunbar to be nearer his daughter, Joyce, with whom he lived for 43 years. Latterly he moved to Hollytrees Nursing Home in Belhaven Hospital in 2007. Jock died in Dunbar, on September 29th, 2008, at the age of 105.

Awards and honours

As well as receiving the Military Medal Jock received the Légion d'honneur, a prestigious military award of France, from the French ambassador, Gérard Errera at the 60th anniversary commemorations. In 1998, Jock was awarded the 'Our Forces Hero' award from the Daily Record and dedicated it to the soldiers who lost their lives on D-Day in Normandy. In 2004 Jock attended the opening of the Scottish Parliament.

On reaching his 100th birthday he received a telegram from the Queen and received another congratulatory letter on his 105th birthday.

Andrew Mcneil 2000 – 2005
Footballer

I attended Leith Academy from 2000 – 2005. I actually really enjoyed Maths as I picked it up really easily. It was funny because I struggled with maths in primary and was in the lower end classes but when I came here the teachers really pushed me and I did really well and progressed to Higher Maths. I studied Physics as well. Mr Hardwick was a good teacher and I really liked him because he was funny. He was a really interesting character who made the subject fun to learn. He used to amaze me with his calculator skills. He was also a big man and seemed physically intimidating (even though he wasn't) and that helped to keep people in line. I had a few different maths teachers and recall Miss Johnston who I liked because she was a strong teacher. She was fiery and quite good fun. I think when classes are kept in order it makes it easier for people to go about their business and learn.

Other subjects I liked – I was quite lucky because I got to choose different subjects in between my Standard Grades and Highers. I took PE, Art and Graphics Higher which was quite good because it is quite hard work doing maths and English but these subjects I could relax in.

Achievement wise, I think I realise now that it is important to get qualifications but at the time I was desperate to leave school and get a job and play football. My Mum encouraged me to stay on for the whole of 5th year as I could have left in January due to my birth date. I did have an offer from a club when I was 16 and still in 5th Year but my Mum talked me out of it as it would have been stupid to have left at this stage. I am glad that I got a good grounding here and qualifications before getting a job. There was a right mixed bag of people that I went to school with and there was also a good mix of teachers from different walks of life which helped to set me up for life. I think Mr McAulay (Headteacher at the time) did a great job. I did have a few run-ins with him but I did think he was a good Headteacher. He would reinforce the school uniform and I understand why he did want us all to wear a uniform.

I only had 2 punishment exercises in the time I attended Leith Academy which I think isn't too bad. I really enjoyed both trips to Benmore. We did a lot of good trips with the school. We also went to Beamish with the History department which was fantastic. We had a really good Football Team and in my last year of school (5th year) we won the East of Scotland Shield which was great. I actually sat my last exam on the same day as the game and when it was over I was finished at school which was a really fitting way to end my school days – being successful, winning a trophy and being with all your friends. Mr McAulay and Mr Mason both took the team and they were both really good men. Mr Mason was also my PE teacher so it was just a really good way of finishing school off.

I have always played football from the age of six or seven years old and things just progressed from there. When I was about 12 years old people started to take an interest in me which was a big deal. I remember the first time I played down south for Blackburn Rovers. It's huge in respect of when I was younger I was a Hibernian fan and had a season ticket to watch them and would have done anything to play for Hibs but suddenly these teams down south were interested in me. When I was 13 years old there I was going down for a trial with Manchester United which was a really big deal but I didn't realise it at the time as I was too young to fully understand it all as it just seemed like an adventure. The last few years at school were quite difficult, especially 5th Year because I had to take a lot of time out of school as I was going with Scottish school boys down to play for Arsenal and Southampton and could only take 4 Highers because of it. I ended up playing for Southampton for 2 ½ years which was very difficult leaving home at the age of 16. During school holidays I did a Sports Academy at Leith Academy whilst taking my Highers. I then got a 6 months contract with Hibernian which was a great opportunity and was good because I moved back home. Eventually I spent 3 ½ years with Hibs and played 45 games for the first team which included the League Cup in 2007. One of the best bits of playing for Hibs was being back in Leith and knowing everyone but it was a bit close to home in respect of when everything was going well for Hibs there weren't any problems but if things were not going well people think they can talk to you about where Hibs were in the League which could make it difficult for normal day living. However, overall it was a pleasant experience. On leaving Hibs I played for Montrose for a year which was great for my career. It was a hard year playing for the 1st Division and I was the main goal keeper and played 30 odd games for them often in poor conditions. It was certainly a great learning experience. Then I moved to Raith Rovers, a 1st division club, who are progressing well and are looking to consolidate their position in the League and perhaps go out to the SPL.

Has fame changed you?

I don't think fame has changed me in a negative way but there is a sort of paranoia that goes with the territory. There are situations that can be awkward and I tend to steer away from them.

What advice would you give current Leith Academy pupils with regard to making it in the world of football?

I remember in 1st year Mr Peat and Mrs Fisher both laughed when I told them that I wanted to be a professional footballer. They both told me the pros and cons of the business and advised me of how hard it would be with only a slim chance of making it. I know that they were not being horrible and they were offering me good advice but I knew I could make it as it was desperately what I wanted.

On the other hand, my first instinct is to tell young people it is a lot of hard work and sometimes with little reward and the competition is huge. However all I have ever wanted to be was a footballer and I wouldn't be deterred by anyone. The advice I would give to young people would be to follow their dreams but make sure they do well at school so that they have something to fall back on in later life. I thankfully worked hard at school and was fortunate to get some Highers that have helped me to access a Sports Coaching college course that will offer me more career options.

What is your biggest achievement?

It would have to be – in 2006 I was playing for the Scottish under 19s and we got to the European Championships which made our team the 1st team to qualify for the World Cup. That was a fantastic achievement because although football is particularly big in this country we aren't particularly good at. We played Spain in the final and we lost 2-1 to them and they were better than us and had players that were being paid millions of pounds but it was a fantastic achievement just to compete with them - not that I felt that way at the time but I can see it for what it is now. Winning the League Cup with Hibs was great but not quite the same as playing with and against some of the best players in the world. Also playing in front of 30,000 Hibs supporters watching and cheering you on and at the end Sun Shine on Leith playing by the Proclaimers comes close!

The future

I want to keep playing and doing well for Raith Rovers and hope that we get promoted to the SPL. I would also like to get back into full time football.

As I am currently doing a Sports Coaching course at college I hope this will open doors for me possibly into a degree or post graduate course. Later in life this should allow me to become a personal trainer, stay in sport and give something back to younger people.

Tony Singh

Leith Academy 1982 – 1986
Owner of Oloroso restaurant in Edinburgh

What did you do when you left school?

As soon as I left school I went on to a Youth Training Scheme. I think the country was in a recession so I went to Scottish and Newcastle – where the Scottish Parliament is sited now. From there I have spoken at Parliament to focus groups and interest groups. I then went to Le Monde pub then I went to Telford College so I worked full time and studied at the same time.

What or who was your inspiration?

Home Economics at Leith academy – it was really good and I loved it. However, as a boy, it was a thing I kept under wraps. I actually won a prize at the school's Awards Evening but it was so un-cool for me to win it that I didn't attend to collect the award! It was un-cool to be successful in my peer group.

Has success changed you?

No, success hasn't changed me and I still keep up with some of my peer group – one of my friends, Richard Ross, is a chef in New Zealand and I still see him. A lot of people in my year group left school early (S4) but have done really well for themselves. The other ones, who followed the academic route and stayed on to S6 still got jobs and are doing well in them, but perhaps these jobs are a bit more 'boring' as I'd see them for me as my job allows me to be creative.

Inspirational teachers

My Home Economics, Chemistry, Physics and History teachers were very inpsirational. I really enjoyed these classes and did well at them

I had a great time when I was at school. You could bunk off and no one reported you. Now parents get a phone call and it's all logged; it's changed days. I send my children to Portobello – arch enemies eh!

There are many more opportunities for pupils these days. Up until S2 teachers could give pupils the belt and Tony recalls a number of teachers who were really strong disciplinarians and you just wouldn't mess with them!

Fun memories

At woodwork and metal work we used to make weapons of all kinds - I don't think you're allowed to do that now! In Home Economics, we had to do sewing, which was just painful, blanket stitch and everything! As kids you read comics and imagined if anyone sat on a needle they'd just jump straight back up. We threaded a darning needle and put it on my mate's seat. He sat straight down on it and we ended up pulling it out of his left buttock by its thread. It was fun for us but not so much fun for him! In Chemistry we used to bring milk and tea bags in, the labs were really big and old fashioned. Unknown to the teacher we used to boil water in beakers at the back of the classroom (health and safety now – eh? Who knows what these beakers were used for?) and make a cup of tea for us all – the teacher never noticed.

Unless you were academic the school seemed quite elitist, again changed days now. At sport you had a couple of guys who did rugby and if you weren't good, you'd get some nasty tackles. In my day even getting to play a musical instrument seemed elitist. I was quite good at playing the flute but I never got on with my music teacher so I didn't get picked. Some staff thought I was a disruptive pupil (allegedly!). You had to buy your own instrument back then so if you weren't so well off you couldn't do these things.

Only a few boys selected Home Economics. I also took Modern Studies (but I never got it at all!).

Tony says he has put in 22 years of hard work to create his restaurant and to get to where he is today. He won a competition - IT Chef of the Year and set up the restaurant on Royal Yacht Britannia.

Motivation, passion and drive have helped Tony get to where he is. Everyone seems to be doing well at school now and along with all the extra-curricular activities pupils need to be able to do what they say they can do as many over promise and under deliver. A lot of young people have the talk these days but confidence and hard work are more important. Also, for young people, this culture of wanting fame just for the sake of wanting to be famous is really worrying. It is really important that both time and talent combine together and this is nurtured. This is what makes success.

Tony talks about the principles of Sikhism being work hard for a living and share what you have. He lives by this ideology. He also remains as positive as he can in his work and remains true to himself. He is who he is and in 2000 he was offered the opportunity to do more TV programmes but they said he would have to get elocution lessons. Tony said 'no' as he likes his dialect. Now they want regional accents but also want you to look younger. Tony laughs, he just can't win. However, he knows he is good at what he does.

Tony has got his inspiration for his food from everywhere - his granny, dad, everybody, people he works with.

He was recently in conversation with people at a business meeting and they asked where he went to school, knowing what he was doing, he said, the Academy, they immediately said 'that's great! Then he followed it up with, that is, Leith Academy, the better one of the two!

Tony Singh's Farm Lamb With Scotch pie

Ingredients

For the jellified lamb stock:
5 kg roughly chopped lamb bones
500grm diced onion
250 grm each diced celery and carrot
100 grms. tomato puree
150 grms fresh thyme
50 grms rosemary
6 bay leaf
50 mls vegetable oil

For the Pie Filling:
2 x large carrots washed and peeled from the garden
2 x Onion peeled from the garden
1 x boned shoulder of Hogget, 2kg/4lb 8oz
45mls x vegetable oil for sealing
100g x bay leaves from the garden 100g x rosemary from the garden
2 tablespoons fresh thyme from the garden
200 g x Peas from the garden
3 Lt x strong jellified brown lamb stock
200 g x of Diced cooked carrot and celery
Salt to taste
Pepper to taste

For the hot water paste:
200g x Lard
120mls x Milk
120mls water
450g x Flour Plain
1 Teaspoon Salt

For the vegetables:
8 x carrots washed peeled
200ml of water with salt to taste
50 grams of caster sugar
100 grams of unsalted butter
8 x nice turned potatoes (200 grams goose)

For the Lamb:

4 x 100g of loin of lamb pieces, de-barked and with a nice bit of fat on them Farm

120mls of reduced cooking stock from the Hogget shoulder

250g x , Peas from the garden cooked in a little butter then mashed with salt, pepper and 5g of finely chopped mint from the garden

4 x 50ml/2fl oz individual Scotch pies (recipe below)

1x egg yolk for glazing

Method

For the jellified lamb stock:

1. Place bones in a roasting pan and place in a 200 degree c oven. Cook until the bones are nicely browned and not at all burned. You will have to keep moving the bones to achieve this

2. In a large pan sauté the onions, celery, and carrots in the oil until lightly browned

3. Add tomato puree and cook for 10 minutes. Be careful not to let the tomato puree burn on the bottom of the pan. Place bones in a stock pot and cover with cold water (fill with enough water to cover bones by 2 inches). Bring to a boil over moderately high heat. Skim scum and reduce heat to a simmer. Add onions, carrots, celery, and tomato puree mixture to the stock pan. Add the herbs. Simmer 5 hours keep skimming off the scum and fat that come through to the top of the stock pot very 20 minutes

4. Strain the stock through a fine strainer and then reduce to the strength you want, pass again and chill use whenever you want.

For hot water paste:

1. In a medium saucepan, bring the water, milk and lard to the boil

2. In a bowl sieve the flour, salt together; make a well in the centre of the bowl

3. Pour in the boiling liquid

4. Mix with a spoon until it is cool enough to do it by hand

5. Mix to a nice soft dough and keep in the bowl with a hot damp tea towel over it

For the hogget filling:

1. Cut the vegetable into 3 ½ inch chunks

2. Season the shoulder thoroughly with salt and fresh milled black pepper

3. In a large pan heat up the oil

4. Seal the meat in the pan and colour it evenly all over

5. Take out the lamb and put it in the Vacuum pack pouch with the herbs

6. Place all the vegetables in the pan and cook on a high heat to give them some colour.

7. Then spoon them into the bag with the hogget shoulder.

8. Place in the jellified lamb stock and seal

9. Cook at 80degrees c for 14 hours in a huge pan

10. Take out the bag from the bath and allow to cool enough so you can handle the meat

11. Cut the bag open drain and reserve the liquid in the bag
12. Discard all the vegetables and the herbs
13. Pick down the shoulder in to nice small pieces not to small as you want some texture to the pie. , put in a bowl to one side
14. Put the reserved stocks from the bag into a pan bring to the boil and skim of any fat, taste and adjust seasoning.
14. Add the diced carrot and celery to the picked lamb and enough of the stock to moisten, check seasoning and put to one side.

For the roast potatoes:
1. Preheat the oven to 220C/425F/Gas 7.
2. Turn the potatoes. Parboil in boiling salted water for 2 minutes. Drain
3. Put 200 grams goose fat in a roasting tin and put in oven, for 8 minutes carefully take the tin out of the oven and add the potatoes to the hot fat, basting them as you do so. Put the tin back in the oven and cook for about 5 to 12 minutes basting and turning them very 3 minutes until the potatoes are golden and crunchy on the outside and soft in the middle.

For the carrots:
1. Take your 8 trimmed carrots and place in 200 mls of water with salt to taste and 50 grams of caster sugar, and 100 grams of unsalted butter.
2. Bring to the boil and simmer until the carrots are just under done.
3. Take the pan of the heat and let the carrots finish cooking in the residual heat of the water.
4. Use the carrots when cold from the pan.

For the pie:
1. For the pie, roll out the paste until it is 3mm thick.
2. Line four buttered 50ml/2fl oz individual pie moulds with the rolled paste
3. Spoon in the Hogget filling and cover with a pastry top and brush with egg yolk
4. Place the moulds on to aroasting tray
5. Bake in the oven for 21 minutes at 185 C.
6. While the pies are cooking get the lamb and other ingredients ready to finish the dish
7. Allow to cool slightly before removing the pies from the mould.

For the lamb:
8. In a large oven proof dish melt the fat and when the pan is hot brown the lamb loins. Season with salt and pepper and finish them by putting them in a preheated oven at 200c until medium rare. The time will depend on the meat you are using but it will probably be about 4 to 6 minutes, take out and leave to rest
9. On warm plates spoon on some bashed peas, two turned potatoes just off center , two nice carrots and a pie on each, Slice a piece of lamb per portion and spread on the plate finish with some of the reduced stock from the cooking of the shoulder

Tony Singh's Rhubarb and Custard

Ingredients

For the custard:
600mlsdouble cream
100mls milk
100g caster sugar
12 egg yolks
1 vanilla pod

For the rhubarb:
Juice 2 Lemons
500g x 2 cm diced rhubarb
500g Sweet cicely
1 litre x Barr's Red Kola

For the jelly:
800mls x Rhubarb cooking liqueur
6 sheets Gelatin soaked in cold water
250g x Pixie strawberry
200g x Pixie strawberry washed and hulled
28 x dried Rhubarb crisps (rhubarb sliced very thinly in to 4 inch lengths dipped in stock syrup then dried on non stick trays over night in a hot cupboard)

For the biscuits:
400 g flour
200 g unsalted butter, at room temperature
1 egg
200 g darkest brown sugar you can get
60g Powdered Molasses or powdered dark brown sugar
15 g full Fat Milk
2 g Table Salt
½ tsp cinnamon
½ tsp ginger
½ tsp gratings of nutmeg

Method

For the custard:
1. Cream yolks and sugar till pale in colour
2. Singe cream and Milk with split pod – (bring to a rapid boil and take off the heat)
3. Pour onto eggs and pour into a clean pan.
4. Cook out on a medium, heat do not boil. As this will curdle the eggs and ruin the custard
5. Pass and mould through a fine sieveto remove the vanilla pod into a bow
6. Cover bowl with cling film and allow to Cool

For the ginger biscuits:
1. Preheat oven to 180 c.
2. Combine the butter, sugar, spices and eggs. In a large mixing bowl add the flour in batches, and knead the dough until it comes together and is smooth dough
3. Cut the dough into two.

4. Lay down a sheet of parchment paper and roll (with rolling pin) one half of your dough as thinly as you can, about **3 mm**, keeping the surface smooth
5. Cut your dough into thin long rectangles
6. Put In Deep Freeze till hard about 1 hour then take out.
7. Carefully using a knife or thin spatula slide the rectangles onto a baking sheet with parchment leaving a small gap between each,
8. Bake for 12 to 15 minutes lift off and cool on wrack

For the rhubarb:
1. Bash the sweet cicely with a rolling pin to reseal the flavours
2. Place all the Ingredients in a Vacuum pouch and seal
3. Cook in a water bath at **62 degrees c** for 1 hour then take out and allow to cool
4. Cut open the bag and strain and reserve the liquid and pick out all the rhubarb you can discard the sweet cicely
5. Pass the liquid through double muslin and we will use this for the jelly

For the jelly:
1. Bring the liquor up to 75 c in a pan on a medium heat **Check for Sweetness**
2. Squeeze out the gelatine and put in to the hot liquid
3. Allow to cool in the pan
4. Reserve 50 g of the strawberry for garnish and chop up the rest roughly
5. Divided the chopped strawberries by 4 and place in the bottom of the glasses for the desert
6. Pour in just enough jelly to just come to the top of the chopped strawberries and place in the fridge till set
7. Place the remaining jelly in a bowl that will fit on another bowl with iced water in it to cool it down, slowly stir this until it starts to thicken, when it does fold in the reserved diced rhubarb and pour into the glasses with the strawberries
8. Place back in the fridge and leave to set
9. When set top off the glasses with the custard and place back in the fridge for 2 hours

To serve:
To serve take out the glasses and place a pile of strawberries in the center of the custard and stick in the biscuits and rhubarb crisps in an abstract way over the strawberries

War Heroes of Leith Academy

Glynn Mullen, a S2 pupil, has been researching the backgrounds of those pupils from Leith Academy who lost their lives in the Second World War from 1939-1945.

Glynn's interest in the pupils from Leith Academy who died in the Second World War came about when he noticed there was no official remembrance board in the school for them. Although former pupils who died in the First World War have one, there is only a plaque to signify the later conflict. Glynn hopes to replace our current Board of Remembrance with a new one that honours them by name.

Since November 2009 Glynn has researched 75 names to date and completed further research on 15 of these men. He set about finding out which pupils went to war, but never came back, eventually gathering the names of all 75 men, as well as autobiographical material about them. His research involved old school registers, a book of remembrance donated to the school by South Leith Parish Church in the 1950s, visits to cemeteries and much communication with the Commonwealth War Graves Commission. He has also met with relatives of the deceased, and now knows where the men lived in Leith, some details about their families, where and how they died, as well as where they are buried.

Below is one of the interviews with relatives of a Leith Academy pupil who fought in WW2 and was killed in action.

Peter Peters
Address: 2 Springfield Street
Left school: 1926
Died: 20th January 1944

Peter served initially with the Royal Scots but was deemed not fit for service due to an injury to his trigger finger he had since childhood. Olive Peters, his sister, describes this as Whitlow finger. Whilst convalescing in hospital Peter witnessed the horrific injuries that soldiers were returning home with and felt he needed to do more. Peter requested a transfer and was later sent to Italy. When in Italy Peter transferred from the Royal Scots to the Argyll and Southern Highlanders.

The main fighting in Italy had ceased by the date of Peter's death but there were still some pockets of resistance from snipers. Officers asked for volunteers to retrieve the body of a fallen soldier who had been killed by sniper fire hours before. Peter volunteered without hesitation and set out to recover the body of the 18 year old soldier. Peter was never to return. Miss Peters described that at the cemetery in Orvieto Peter is laid next to the soldier who he tried to recover.

Olive described Peter as a popular boy who was "handsome but not conceited" and "witty without being cruel"

While at school Peter excelled at Maths and disliked Latin saying he didn't like his Latin teacher.

Olive says that if Peter hadn't joined the forces he would have made a good script writer for comedy.

Obituary notices

Peters, *remembering with pride and affection, my devoted fiancé Peter. (8thJune 1944) Killed in action Italy June 6th 1944* **Annie Hallewell**

(Annie never married after Peters death)

Peters *Mr and Mrs Thoms Peters 23 Prospect Bank Crescent Edinburgh that their beloved younger son Peter was killed in action in Italy June 1944 He is fondly remembered. His parents wish to thank all friends for kind letters, cards and sympathy received.*

Harold Swanston

Jock Wilson's nephew (one of our notable alumni), Wing Commander Harold Swanston, also a former pupil of Leith Academy, died in active service during WW2. He was the highest ranking officer from all the former pupils to die in active duty during WW2 in 1944. He died when he boarded a Lancaster Mark III Bomber (serial No ND905) to attack the great German tank depot at Mailly, on the night of 3/4 May 1944. This aircraft was one of a force of 346 Lancasters, sent to bomb a German military camp near the village of Mailly-le-Camp. Of the 346 Lancasters 42 failed to return to base. It was later reported that Lancaster ND905 had crashed and exploded, with the loss of all seven crew members, near Chalons Sur-Marne. The probable cause was that it had been shot down by a German night fighter.

Ken Hyslop
Headteacher 1983-1994

I arrived from my time at Castlebrae High, a school serving a deprived area in 1983. I was immediately struck by the fact that Leith pupils were suffering from a different form of deprivation, one no less damaging. Leith pupils were seriously deprived of a school building capable of giving them an equal chance of success compared to others in Edinburgh. They were taught in three different buildings one at least a mile distant from the "main school".

What this meant was that the first and second years were taught in the junior school (the old Norton Park secondary). Many staff travelled up and down Easter Road to fulfil their timetable commitments. Others were permanently based there and taught only S1 and S2, not a desirable situation for the development of a career. For the pupils this was not an acceptable situation for a number of reasons. These children were deprived of the experience of the full range of their peer group, 12 to 18. They were deprived of experiencing the continuum of the education process in secondary. They met a narrower group of teachers than would be desirable. All in all they were experiencing a poor deal as compared to other pupils in Scotland.

The main school was not on one site either but consisted of two buildings, separated by two major roads. This meant that pupils spent ages travelling to and fro across these roads during their timetabled day. Both buildings, but particularly the Lochend Annexe, were in a very poor state of repair. The playing fields were a mile away at Hawkhill which again had pupils travelling up and down for PE.

All of these obstacles greatly disadvantaged the pupils and the staff. For that reason I felt we must act to alert those in power to this unacceptable situation. The School Council agreed we should make our discontent known. Quickly we enlisted support from the staff, the parents, local politicians, public meetings, etc., a fair bit of luck, we succeeded and a new school over at Academy Park was agreed.

We were again in luck. An architect new to the region had a particularly strongly held view that we should break the mould of traditional school design and try to create something different, exciting and inspiring to the users of the building. We know that she succeeded spectacularly in this aim.

Together, with her leadership we set about the design. A piazza running through the centre of the school with a street café and plants on either side. Thereafter the School departments would be arranged on either side of the street. This was done with the specific plan of linking areas of the curriculum together. The library, computer studies and business studies, information technology being linked; aesthetic subjects, art, music and drama etc; science and technology and so on. A further clear ideal in the design was to make the learning process visible. Windows on the street into departments would reveal to passers-by what each subject offered. It was described as shopping for education while walking in the street.

We moved over on a weekend and opened on a Tuesday. The change was profound. There can be no argument that the first reaction to the new school was immediately positive. To be all together on one site was marvellous. One school not a series of dilapidated buildings. One body of pupils and one unified body of staff. Immediately noted was the pupil behaviour. They were much calmer in the new environment, more relaxed in the breaks, using the street to meet and chat, using the street café etc.

It was a great campaign and a tremendous victory for the children of Leith. What a memory for me.

Sandy McAulay
Headteacher 1995-2007

Sandy starts by describing the school as having a lovely morale–staff, pupils and parents. He was proud to have been given the role of Headteacher of Leith Academy at a very young age; one of the youngest to have ever been appointed by Edinburgh. He recounts how he was issued with the task of moving the school forward and making significant changes. It is the changes he made over his 13 years at the school that he is proudest of and that he made these changes through the process of consultation; something the school had not been used to in the past. In the first few years as Headteacher there were significant changes in the staff profile and one of the first things that happened was the re-structuring of Pupil Support and Guidance and he used the skills of the Senior Management Team and the wider staff to help make these changes to make a more effective school. Also major changes were made to the structure of the day through the removal of registration and the introduction of Tutor Groups to encourage staff to take on more of a pastoral role at all levels.

The other area Sandy feels he made considerable changes in was the running of the community school. Prior to his arrival the building seemed to be an open house to anyone who wished to visit it and this also meant on occasions that there were some unwelcome guests from time to time and this was disruptive to some of the adult classes running. Sandy approached the council to purchase some extra security for the building and used the £30,000 he got to make the building a safer place for all in it through CCTV cameras and through cordoning off the car park area and playing fields to create a boundary. Sandy recalls one of the difficult visitors he dealt with, who after being abusive to both the janitors and himself, left the building after major resistance. As the man left the building and Sandy had thought he had 'seen the back of him' he turned to walk back up the corridor of the school to meet with the janitors. As he did so he could see smoke coming from his head. He then found a lit cigarette in the hood of his anorak, which the man must have flicked in his hood when Sandy had turned to walk back in to the building. Sandy can now see the funny side of this but I can imagine that smoke was really coming out his ears at the time! Sandy also recounts being challenged to a fight in his first year at Leith Academy. As there was no uniform at the time he didn't know whether this person was a pupil or not and here he was, being challenged to a square go! He was thinking 'this is some place'! Sandy was able to reason with him and diffuse the situation and managed to ensure this person left the premises. However what this did highlight was with 13 different entry points around the building security measures were needed as was a school uniform – and this was another of Sandy's successful changes and the school has made major ground in this area. This would give the school an identity and togetherness – we are all in it together. Sandy got the pupils and staff involved in leading this and the pupils wanted both a junior and senior uniform and again, Sandy remarks that only a few schools had started to consider the uniform route and here again, we were a school leading the way – as we had done in many areas. This was great for the school as Leith Academy had not been viewed in this way.

Sandy also reminisces about his Friday break time chats. These were not only the opportunity to celebrate success but also an occasion to poke some fun at himself. It allowed staff to gather together and reflect on the week's events.

Sandy discusses how the good work at Leith Academy is just more than league tables or attainment statistics as much of the good work that a school does is not measurable and this is why he was so disappointed in the initial HMIe report in 2008, as it did not reflect the school which he had led and managed for 13 years. The parents of Leith Academy pupils are very caring parents and we welcomed their engagement in working together in raising attainment and the more we can get on board with us the better this attainment will get.

As Headteacher Sandy is proud of the opportunities he afforded for staff to develop professionally throughout their careers at Leith Academy. He set up secondment opportunities to SMT so that PTs could become more familiar with the leadership and management decisions made in regard to taking the school forward. It was about making the leadership more transparent and bringing staff on board with the decision making. If he had a legacy at all, it would be the empowerment of staff and he knows that those in the current SMT also recognise the importance of this.

When asking Sandy to recall some of his funniest moments one immediately springs to mind for him. It was a readmission meeting for a pupil following their exclusion. The parents of the pupil had arrived unannounced having missed the original readmission meeting but Sandy agreed to see them. During the meeting the father sat quietly chewing gum and the mother did all the talking for them both stating that her son was the victim in the whole situation. Whilst Sandy was setting out the terms for the readmission, the dog 'let off' and it was one of the longest, loudest passing of wind Sandy had ever heard from any being and the smell was unbelievable, like an elephant had dropped something in his room. Well, the interview went on amid all this guff and nobody said anything. Sandy couldn't laugh and he had to continue the meeting as it was of a serious nature but still couldn't believe that the parents hadn't heard the dog let off. At the end of the meeting when they all left and the dog went out he had to fumigate his room. What Sandy was more worried about that he hadn't sufficient time to rid his room of the pungent smell before his next visitor and them thinking it was him! Sandy said there were many awkward moments like that but you just have to laugh or you would crack up.

One of the highlights for Sandy was taking the Senior Football Team away to the Scottish Cup and beating Beeslack in the final. It was good to be able to share this moment with Fraser Mason and the S5/6 team.

Sandy talks about the great times and the great laughs he had with the kids; the Charity work the school did and the sponsored walk and how these things are part and parcel of what makes a great school - when staff and pupils work together. He remarks on the generosity of spirit you get from the community at large and the responsibility given to the senior pupils to manage such things and how this makes for effective partnership working.

There was only one day a year Sandy wished he could find something else to do. That was the day that the seniors left the school – May 31st! This was the day that the flour and eggs came into play and there were a few years things got out of hand. Once the pupils got the idea to go away from the school, to the Links that was better. However, he stresses that we have so many good seniors. Sandy also changed the format of the Evening of Celebration to embrace successes in both achievement and attainment and this also changed the ethos of the school. His reason for doing this was he wanted to celebrate a truly comprehensive community school and to make it a celebration of all pupils' achievements in the widest sense.

In the last few minutes of Sandy's interview he discussed how he misses Leith Academy hugely and how he sometimes wished he was still sitting at his desk.

I am sure all staff who worked with Sandy will agree with me in saying that he gave his all to Leith Academy - he was an all or nothing person and never did anything by half. Everything he could do for the school he did and he leaves his legacy with us in all the many changes and great work he did here.

Odd Ode

In spite of all her diet sheet said,
Poor Tessie was inclined to spread,
Instead of being skin and bone,
She tipped the scales at twenty stone.
You can imagine how this got her,
So many times into hot water,
But this last phrase though somewhat terse,
In bathing pools was in reverse.

One day at Portobello Pool,
She eyed the shimmering water cool,
Assumed a most superior bend,
And dived in at the deepest end.
But though her style was most aquatic,
Alas! Results were most dramatic,
Spectators at the side were damped,
And swimmers in the pool were swamped.

In face so mighty was the race,
That some were found at Largo Place,
An alarmed attendant shouted, "Coo,
No need for me to start waves noo!"
A half-drowned man was heard to quip,
"They've gone and sunk a battle ship!"
When Tessie asked to make amendment,
She was dragged before the superintendent,
He stared amazed, then: "Jings," said he,
"Looks like a blinkin'whale to me!"

So, poor Tessie got the job,
Of making waves to suit the mob,
Of course her dives they regulate,
In case she drowns those who spectate.

PAT SUTHERLAND (3A1) 1960

A Leith Tiger

Gleaming eyes like flashing lights,
Unblinking, yellow, round,
Watching a gently waving string,
Waiting – without a sound.

Faint quiver in his back and tail;
The rest is stealthy – still,
Alert to every tiny twitch
Of the quarry he must kill.

A leap – too late! He has it fast
Between his fearful jaws,
And now 'tis dead, he can relax,
To wash, and lick his paws.

CAROLYN QUINN (1B4) 1960

A Punter Born in Leith

Every day at lunch time,
You see the kids out for a stroll,
They aren't out for exercise,
They're out to Greggs for a sausage roll.

A favourite sound doon Leith way,
Is the motorists car horn,
Because they've nearly hit another kid,
From Hermie, Leith or Lorne.

There's a lot of pubs down Leith walk,
Which all have their special charms.
It's hard to find a bar quite like,
The Boundary Bar or Volly Arms.

When you head down the seafront,
There are fancy restaurants galore,
But the locals prefer the chippy,
If they are dining at the shore.

When you walk along Great Juction Street,
You'll see someone that you ken,
And there will be lots of women gossiping,
Complaining about their men.

The pubs in Leith are always busy,
With the lads in for a sup,
And you'll always hear somebody say,
Will Hibs <u>ever</u> win the cup?

And of course there's Ocean Terminal,
That place has got the lot!
And it must be pretty special,
As the queen has berthed her yacht.

You'll always see a black eye,
And folk with missing teeth.
But you're sure to get a smile,
From a punter born in Leith.

LAURA BURNS (S1)

I Love Leith

When the sun shines on Leith,
It brings a smile to me,
I love Leith

A smile full of love and joy,
Leith for every girl and boy,
I love Leith,

I can hear people screaming,
I can hear them out loud,
I love Leith,

Leith is for you,
Leith is for me,
I love Leith,
Leith is for us.

LEIGHANNE GANNON (S1)

Sunshine on Leith

When I first walked in the school,
My first impression was cool,
Trees, bushes and plants were everywhere I looked.

In the English room I looked,
Was a classroom full of books.

All I heard was pupils chatting,
And teachers teaching.
Pupils getting hyper,
And teachers getting madder.

Our school is very loved.
By pupils, parents and even seagulls listening to the lesson from above!

A very generous school this is,
By raising money for charities.
Wearing what you want for a pound.
For jeans for jeans and think pink!

AREHA TAHIR (S1)

Olivia (Olive) Henderson (née Proudfoot)
Attended Leith Academy 1927 - 1937

Olivia attended Leith Academy from age 5 years and her first memory of the school that she recalls is the Christmas Party when she saw Santa and heard the sleigh bells.

In those days a piano played whilst all the pupils marched to their classroom. She recalls the school blazer and hat that kept her cosy in the winter. Teachers wore gowns to school. Girls in the A/B classes took French and Latin and the C/D classes took sewing and cooking. *Olive in her Leith Academy school uniform* Primary pupils had mixed sex playtime whereas secondary pupils had single sex playgrounds. Games such as skipping ropes, peevers and chasing games were regular playground games.

Olive recalls a bad memory of her Science class when tadpoles got spilt and boiling water was accidentally poured over them.

Olive left school at 15 years old and could read and write well. The teachers were good at teaching but she remembers them looking ancient even although they were just out of training. Badly behaved pupils got the strap for being cheeky or talking during lessons. Friday afternoon at school was a treat because teachers used to get books out and read – Peter Pan was a favourite of Olive's.

Out of school Olive recalls chores were done unwillingly. She used to go to the store for messages with a shopping list. Olive was pleased that the shops were closed every Wednesday as she didn't need to get messages for her parents. One good thing that came after the war, that Olive recalls, was the queuing crowds at the counter of the shops.

There was no television in those days. People listened to the radio or gramophone. Olive used to read comics such as Bo Peep and would swap these with friends. In the street Olive played games such as Diablo, football and marbles. Olive recalls it being safer playing in the streets in those days as there was less traffic – horse and carts were often used around the streets. She attended Brownies and Guides and recalls the Guide camps she attended. There was more freedom to do things.

Olive shared a bed with 3 siblings and her brother had to sleep on a folding bed in the living room. She lived in a prefab (steel) bungalow with a big garden.

When she was older she would be expected to be home by 10pm or earlier and she and friends would often hide in the hedges when they heard their mothers calling them in.

After WW1 Olive recalls the Great Depression – people were out off work, men would come and sing and children would be sent down with coppers. Leith has changed a lot.

Olive as she is today

Chris Whelan (née Currie)
Attended Leith Academy 1936 -1939

Chris lived in Buchan Street at the border of Leith and Edinburgh with her sister and two brothers who were all much older than her – her sister was 21 years older. She lived in a flat with two bedrooms and bathroom which was unusual as most people in those days had an outside toilet. Her father died when she was 12 years old. From what she remembers her mother didn't work as she suffered with migraines and she would often see her mother go to her room with vinegar on a cloth to ease the pain of the migraine.

Children had more freedom than kids do today. Chris lived in a close knit community and everyone looked out for everyone in the neighbour hood. No supervision was needed and she played in the local streets and at parks at both Iona Street and Dalmeny Street. There were lots of places to play and your parents didn't have to bother about you as everyone knew everyone. When parents did look for you they just needed to ask a neighbour if they'd seen you and they would tell them where you where. She recalls playing games such as football and kerby and other street games with all the local children. She was too busy playing with her friends to join Guide or Brownie clubs.

Chris remembers her favourite toy was a Red Riding Hood doll. She reckons she was a lucky child and possibly spoilt in comparison to other children from bigger families as her mother bought everything new – nothing was handed down or second hand from other people and her mother made a lot of things for her to wear. Other families had a real tough time in comparison to her family who were financially comfortable.

Primary school (Leith Walk Primary) wasn't very strict but you didn't answer teachers back and in those days you had a lot more respect for teachers than kids do today. She received a bursary to attend Leith Academy from Heriot's because her father had died. Chris enjoyed playing sports at school and in her final year she became the Sports Captain and was awarded a watch for her role as this – she doesn't know what she has done with the watch but still has the box which she occasionally shows her Grandchildren. Class numbers were quite big and it was the same age group in each class. She didn't wear a uniform to primary but wore a blazer when she attended Leith Academy. Chris also had a special kit she wore to PE. She recalls one teacher in particular that she liked a great deal as he was a very good PE teacher and played football. She liked mathematics but didn't care for English or other subjects. In those days you had a teacher for two years which helped you have a better relationship with your teacher. Her mother born in 1885 was a very wise clever woman but didn't have much of an education because she left school at 13 years old and was put to work but always encouraged her daughter to work hard at school. She left school at 15 ½ years old as the Second World War started and she no longer had to attend. She can't remember ever doing homework.

Chris didn't need to do many chores around the house when she was at school as her mother took on those responsibilities herself.

Chris remembers receiving one penny per week pocket money on a Friday from her mother but didn't have to earn it by doing chores. She remembers her girlfriends having to help around the house but that was mainly because they had larger families. When she was older she helped around the house as all girls were expected to do. Her brothers never did housework – "boys didn't do such things".

When she was older and started work she had to give her mother her wages and she was then given money to spend on necessities. This stopped eventually when she started to go to the dancing as she had more freedom.

For holidays the family visited family members in Larbert, Falkirk, who lived in the country. They spent a lot of time there – weekends and one week during school holidays. Her aunt kept chickens and she enjoyed her time there. During summer holidays from school she would ride the tram to visit the Open Air Pool at Portobello and go on picnics to Leith Links. Every Saturday she enjoyed visiting the cinema to see the latest Saturday morning cliffhanger.

Her son was involved in Leith Academy's 400th Anniversary as he attended Leith Academy and played in the School Brass Band. He was involved in the cine footage that Leith Academy took.

Chris has two grandsons who attended Leith Academy until recently and looks after them on occasions.

Jim Collie
(local resident and brought up in Leith)

I lived in Albert Street at the top of Easter Road. There was Mum, Dad – nine of us altogether. My grandparents were Berwickshire people so they didn't live with us. I had two older brothers and four sisters – all in a room and kitchen. We'd be sleeping under beds, in bunk beds, ten to a bed! Mum and Dad's bed was up on blocks and there'd be another below it which pulled out. Every space was taken at night. I think they were glad when I went away to the Army – it gave more space. At least we had an inside toilet. There would be all nine of us at night, sitting round the gas fire and with one light. Sometimes we'd listen to the radio – the battery went to get charged every few days and my brother Archie would be sitting reading.

I went to Albion Road Primary School but it changed from a primary to a secondary and so I went to Lorne Street Primary. When I left Lorne Street I went back to Albion Road and while I was there they changed it to Norton Park. What do I remember about Primary? Can I tell you a story? When I went from Albion Road to Lorne Street, I remember I went into the room: there were forty in the classes in those days. The teacher said, "Just sit down there just now," so I sat right at the front. An hour and a half later I heard her ask someone to clean the blackboard and I thought it was me. She said, "You clown, you clown" and that was me for the rest of Primary: "Clown Collie!" I was the clown and my brother was a professor. Archie was dux of the school. I was about six years old then – can you believe it?

School was quite strict. Many of the teachers were at the end of their careers. Young ones were away at war. Those left seemed to be old buddies, perhaps they should have been retired but had to stay on because the young folk had gone to fight. They all used the belt - there were no canes - just the belt. Everyone got it except for a few clever ones, even some of the lassies. And of course there were lines. Teachers used to ask you to stand up and read and then ask if words were nouns or verbs. If you said, "I dinnae ken," you would have got the strap.

Lessons were basic: English, Mathematics, History and Geography, never anything other than the basics. I wasnae bad at any of them, but I wasnae great at any of them either. My brother Archie was called "the Professor". He was in and out of the library up at Albert Street every other day. He'd sit there reading his books and get three or four out at a time. My next brother, Dod, used to think he was more clever than Archie, but they didn't accept that at school because Archie, he was the bees' knees.

My parents were country people: Dad came from Paxton in Berwickshire and Mum from Edrington Castle and Edrington Mill. I suppose their attitude towards school was just "behave yourselves!" If you got the strap, you got the strap. Not like nowadays. You left school at fourteen – the only ones who stayed on were a few clever ones but they went to Broughton. One older sister went to Broughton and learned Latin. She learned all the fancy Latin words and then ended up working in a newsagent's. Ha!

My dad was a country person at first and there was a horse and cart place called Cowan's. He used to bring horses up for Cowan's to buy and someone must have said did he not fancy a job in Edinburgh and we lived at 91 – next to the main entrance of Cowan's. The Railway was involved in someway and first he had a job as a carter, then a lorry driver. My mum never had a job outside the family – it was enough bringing up seven of us. We had to be careful with money of course. I sometimes wondered how they managed. My dad was away a lot and Mum had a hell of a job trying to cater for everyone: Archie didn't like milk and with Dad it was onions… so she was always having to do different things for different ones. As far as clothes went it was a lot of hand-me-downs. And the woman downstairs was very handy with the sewing machine. Albert Street wasn't a pauper street but everyone was the same: when you'd a big family you had to make do and mend. It was a bit different though when you were older and had a few bob. Wages were still rubbish but at least you had some money and you could get a suit made. If I'd the money now, I'd invest in a denim factory. Everybody wears jeans now!

When we were younger we would be sent down to the Borders in the summer, you know, the River Tweed and all those things that were quite different from a townie. We'd sometimes have days out at Leith Links. And Dad worked for Cowan & Company which was a railway place. We got those privilege tickets and could travel on the trains for a couple of coppers. That was good. Then when we were older we'd go cycling and camping. Later on you might start with the Isle of Man or Ireland. A lot of kids never got away. I suppose it was to do with the war years as well.

We'd sometimes go to the baths, and I played football till I was quite old, and for the Scottish Select – until I realised I'd never make the big time. Every spare minute we'd be out kicking a ball. Then at night in the winter we'd meet in people's houses and play cards. Later on when I stopped football I took up golf and I enjoyed that. Some folk went ice skating at Haymarket and then Murrayfield, but it was considered a snob's game. Can ye imagine going along Albert Street with a pair of skates? We'd find a pair of skates in the pawn shop.

You could also go down to Newhaven fishing off the pier end or swimming in the harbour. At one time you could have crossed the harbour by stepping on one boat after another, that's how close they were. They're not there now. When we were young the shore was tidal and the shipyards had to wait for the tide when they were launching the ships. They've done away with the gates and things now – it's all different.

When I left school at fourteen, I started as a wheelwright, making wheels. After a year that ended and I met a pal of mine when I was going to sign on. He worked for Aiken & Wright, a wholesale provision merchant and asked if I wanted a job and I worked there till I got an apprenticeship in 1944. During the war we never wanted for anything – not stealing though. We'd get 2oz of this and 2oz of that, but we didn't suffer for these sorts of things. Clothes were different - everyone was short and had to make do, and children got hand-me-downs.

My apprenticeship was in coach painting. I finished up with the Lothian Coach Works at Tollcross for 50-odd years. I was manager by the time I finished. I didnae hate it but it was just a job – though quite a good job. I must have been half-decent, as when I'd been there a couple of years, there was a pay-off, but they kept me on even though they got rid of folks who'd been there for years. I must have been better than them. I remember all their names: Jimmy, Willie…. I was there until I retired – a long time.

When I met Janet (my wife) she lived in the Corporation Buildings – she was a Leither. We used to go up to Edinburgh to dance at The Palais or The Plaza and all those places. Leith was where the pictures were. The Evening News had a list of what was on every night, at all the pictures. There was lots of dancing and going to the pictures.

Yesterday when I was at the Baths with my daughter, Vicky, I remembered that next to that was where the Swanfield Flour Mill was. Leith has changed a lot since then – even Leith Academy was across the road. Lorne Primary is still there and Norton Park used to be an annexe for Leith Academy. Everything is different now in Leith – you get far more people from all over the place. The younger generation are all different nowadays. When I see the kids coming out from Leith Academy, for instance – it was a "posh" school in those days. Lorne Street was ordinary but Leith Academy and Broughton were a different class.

I'm not sure that life is easier now. It just annoys me that I'm getting to the end of it! Someone was talking about coming to the school here in October 2010 for the celebrations and I was thinking that maybe I'll not be here by then. However I am keeping fit so I hope to be there!

Leith Cuisine

Spring Rolls (a favourite in Home Economics)

Ingredients
10 mls of oil
1 clove garlic (crushed), 1 spring onion, 1/8 red pepper
25gms beansprouts
small piece of ginger
fresh coriander
1 tsp fish sauce
2 spring roll wrappers

Method
Heat the oil – fry the crushed garlic & chopped peppers.
Add the beansprouts, spring onions, ginger, coriander and fish sauce.
Cook stirring until heated through.
Place a spoonful of the mixture down the middle of each spring roll.
Brush the edges with water. Fold the top and bottom over and then fold in the sides to form a sealed roll.
Fry in a deep fat fryer for 2/3 minutes or until golden brown.

Chicken/Quorn in black bean sauce (one of our popular Chinese style dishes and cooked in the past with S5/6 international cookery classes in Personal Development)

Ingredients
1 tablespoon canned black beans
½ onion
½ red pepper
½ green pepper
1 teaspoon cornflour
2 fl oz. Chicken / veg stock
1 teaspoon soy sauce
½ teaspoon sugar
1 tablespoon oil
1 clove garlic – crushed
1 piece chicken / quorn – cut in to strips
50gms long grain rice

Method

Rinse and mash the black beans. Cut the onion into wedges. Cut the peppers into small strips or pieces. Dissolve the cornflour in the stock - add the soy sauce and sugar to this stock also.

Heat the oil gently then add the garlic, onion and peppers – and stir-fry for 1 minute. Add the chicken or quorn and stir-fry for 2 minutes. Add the black beans and the cornflour mix and stir until the sauce thickens. Serve with boiled rice.

Benmore Vegetable Soup

Pupils have the opportunity to spend a week at Benmore Outdoor Centre in S1 and a weekend in S6.

The days are always action packed and the soup and sandwich lunch is very welcome before heading out for afternoon activities.

Vegetable soup

Serves 6

2 medium onions

1 large potato cubed

50g of butter

carrots and a celery bunch (or any vegetable or vegetable combination of your choice)

500ml of stock (stock cubes are fine)

1. Dice onions and cook in butter

2. Cook onions until soft

3. Add the vegetables and potato and stir until they are covered in butter

4. Put the lid on the pan and allow the vegetables cook on a medium heat for 10 minutes.

5. Add 500ml of chicken or vegetable stock and boil until vegetables are soft.

6. The soup can be eaten chunky or blended to create a smooth texture.

Serve with a cheese roll, crisps and a chocolate biscuit.

Leith Links Kebabs

Leith Academy has an African Link with a School in Malawi called St Joseph's Demonstration School. This simple African dish has a lovely tang.

Pork Kebabs

Serves 4

500g Diced pork

Yellow pepper cut into chunks

Mushrooms quartered
Red Onion cubed
100ml malt vinegar
3 gloves of garlic
2 tbsp of cracked pepper

1. Add the marinade : Vinegar, finely chopped garlic and pepper to the pork and leave overnight in the fridge. At the same time put some BBQ skewers in water to soak
2. Using the soaked skewers make up the pork and vegetables kebabs
3. Grill or BBQ the kebabs
Serve with salad and baked potatoes

Prom Dinner
This is a version of the 2010 prom dinner. Chicken in tarragon sauce with mash and green beans.

Chicken and tarragon sauce
Serves 4
Chicken breast (1 per person)
75ml medium dry white wine
150ml chicken stock
150ml double cream
2 tbsp chopped tarragon

Mash potato and green beans
6 large potatoes
100g of butter
Warm milk
500g green beans

Chicken with Tarragon Sauce
1. Heat your oven to 200°C
2. Brown the chicken breast in an oiled pan before placing in a roasting tin.
3. Roast the chicken for about 20 minutes or until the juices are clear.
4. Remove the chicken from the roasting tray, pour off any excess fat and set the chicken breasts aside and keep warm.
5. Add the wine to the roasting tray and reduce it to about 2 tbsps.
6. Add the stock and reduce to a third.

7. Add the cream, bring to the boil and add the chopped tarragon.

8. Plate your chicken and spoon over the tarragon sauce.

Mash potato

1. Cube the potatoes and add to boiling water.

2. Boil for about 20 minutes or until the potato is soft.

3. Mash the potato and add the butter.

4. Add enough warm milk to give a smooth mash

Green Beans

1 Add the green beans to boiling water and blanche for about 3/4 minutes

A Leith Academy Canteen Favourite - Pizza

Pizza is always popular at lunch time. Try making your own with the school's own recipe.

Dough

350g strong white plain flour

7g easy blend yeast sachet

2 tablespoons olive oil

225ml of tepid water

Toppings

Sliced Pepperoni or chorizo sausage

Sliced yellow pepper

½ sliced red onion

6 Sliced mushrooms

1 ball of Mozzarella

200g of cheddar cheese

Tomato sauce

2 red onions

2 tsp Balsamic vinegar

2 tins of tomatoes

5 cherry tomatoes

3 leaves of Fresh Basil

Chilli

2 Garlic cloves

Dough

1. Measure the oil and water in to a large bowl and add the flour and yeast.

2. Knead the mixture for 3 minutes or until the dough is elastic.

3. Leave the dough in clean bowl and cover with Clingfilm.

4. Leave the dough until it doubles in size.

5. Flour your work surface and shape your pizza base

6. Cook your base at 250°C for about 8 minutes or until the base lightly browned.

Tomato Sauce

1½ red onion (the other ½ is used for topping)

2 tsp Balsamic vinegar

2 tins of tomatoes

5 cherry tomatoes

3 leaves of Fresh Basil

1 medium chilli with seeds removed

2 Garlic cloves

1. Blend the tomatoes, basil, garlic, and chilli in a food processor until it has a smooth consistency

2. Add the diced onion to a small oiled pan.

3. Once softened add the Balsamic vinegar.

4. After 2 minutes add the blended mixture and cook on a medium heat for 10 minutes.

Build your Pizza

You are now ready to add your tomato sauce and toppings. Build you pizza and put it in a 220°C oven for 15 minutes or until golden brown.

This is the original emblem of Leith, unveiled after 90 years absence, by the Lord Provost of Edinburgh. (14th September 2010)